D1531182

Drawing
with pencils

Paige Henson

The Rourke Press, Inc.
Vero Beach, Florida 32964

ART CREDITS:
Courtesy of Mr. and Mrs. Clay Elliot, Macon, Georgia: page 5; Keith Heck, Kingfish
Studios: pages 9, 22, 23; © Corel: pages 11, 12; Jon DiVenti, Kingfish Studios:
pages 13, 14, 15, 16, 17, 18, 19, 20, 24, 25; Joseph Pinaud: pages 21, 26, 27, 28;
C. Beyl, Kingfish Studios: page 25; © Eyewire, Inc.: page 8

PHOTOGRAPHY:
Glen Benson and East Coast Studios

PRODUCED & DESIGNED BY:
East Coast Studios, Merritt Island, Florida

EDITORIAL SERVICES:
Susan Albury

ACKNOWLEDGEMENTS:
East Coast Studios would like to thank Gardendale Elementary School, Merritt
Island, for their assistance in this project.

Library of Congress Cataloging-in-Publication Data

Henson, Paige, 1949-
    Drawing with pencils / by Paige Henson
        p. cm. — (How to paint and draw)
    Includes bibliographical references and index.
    Summary: Provides techniques and advice on drawing with pencils and
suggests several projects to try.
    ISBN 1-57103-310-6
    1. Pencil drawing—Technique Juvenile literature. [1. Pencil drawing—
Technique. 2. Drawing—Technique.] I. Title. II. Series: Henson, Paige, 1949-
How to paint and draw.
NC890.H46 1999
741.2'4—dc21   99-30657
                                                                       CIP

Printed in the USA

Contents

CHAPTER 1
The History of Pencils and Paper

Sketching and drawing is often done in preparation for the creation of other art forms such as oil and watercolor painting, sculpture, and architecture. Artists also sketch out their designs for fashions, jewelry, masks, and theatrical sets. In fact, it's difficult to think of a single art form that does not have its beginnings in a drawing or sketch. Still, many people have selected drawing alone as their art of choice.

Of all the drawing tools—charcoal, chalk, crayons, pens, and others—pencils are perhaps the most familiar to you and the easiest to use, because mistakes can be erased. The first wooden pencils, introduced in the early 1800s, had no erasers at their end. They were crude instruments compared to the pencils available today in all shapes, sizes, and colors.

Nearly 2,000 years ago, people from China made the first paper as we know it from mulberry tree bark. Before that time, ancient Egyptians used **papyrus** (puh PIE ruhss), a kind of paper made from woven grass beaten thin. Other items used throughout history for drawing and painting were silk, wood, stone, bark, and specially prepared animal skins.

This looks much like the papyrus used by the ancient Egyptians.

Drawing Materials

Pencils

In pencils made especially for drawing, the lead can be soft, medium, hard, or somewhere in between. Softer pencils have a letter "B" printed on them. Sometimes there is a number before the letter "B." This number tells you how soft the pencil lead is. For example an 8B pencil is much softer than a 2B pencil and will make a darker line that smudges easily. Hard pencils have a letter "H" printed on them. A 6H pencil lead is harder than a 2H pencil lead. Hard pencils are good for drawing fine, precise lines like those in an architect's drawing.

In the photograph below, the top line was drawn with an 8B pencil; the bottom line was drawn with a 4H pencil.

Paper

Smooth paper is good for precise, fine-line drawings. If your drawings are going to be loose and free, with lots of tones and shadings, use a **textured** (TEKS churd) paper.

Other Useful Materials

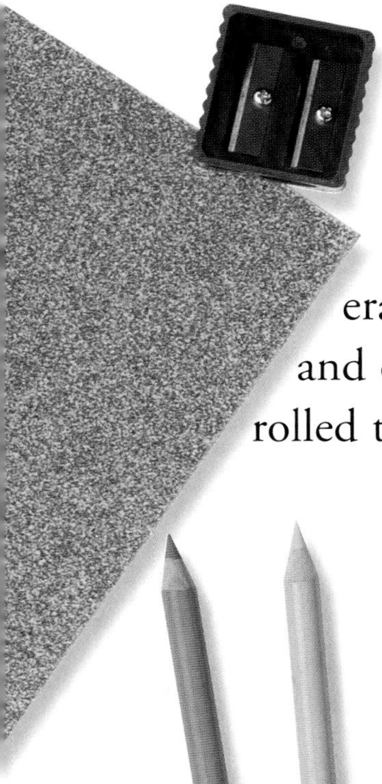

1 A pencil sharpener. Sandpaper is also good for sharpening pencils.

2 A gum eraser or kneaded eraser. A kneaded eraser is soft and can be stretched out or rolled to a point. It won't damage your paper like other erasers will.

3 A set of colored pencils

4 A straight edge

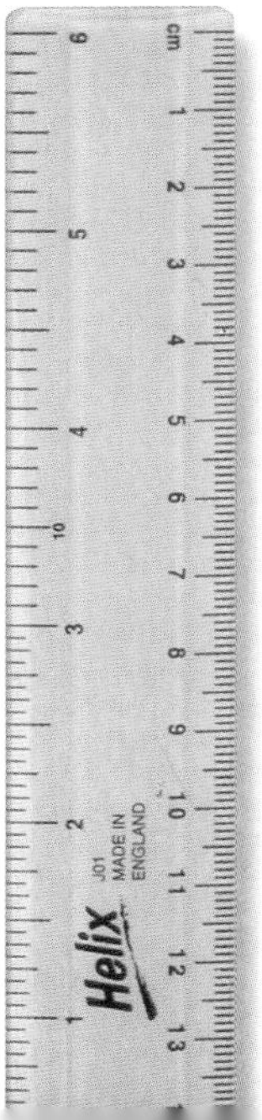

7

Get in the habit of taking a sketch pad and pencil with you everywhere you go to capture the images you might want to draw later. Rough sketches or **thumbnail drawings** (THUHM nayl DRAH ingz) will do—just draw the basic outlines or capture details you want to remember and fill in the rest later. You should also use your sketch pad to paste or clip in photos or designs from magazines, cards, or other printed pieces. Your sketch pad will help you keep all the most interesting visual impressions of your world together in one place. It is a valuable tool for any artist.

Just think! If you become a famous artist, someday your sketchbooks may be on display in museums, like Leonardo da Vinci's.

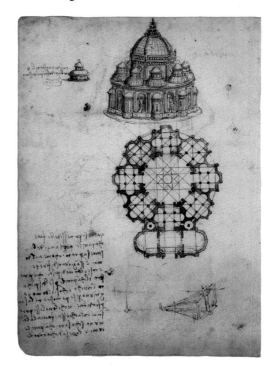

The famous Italian artist, scientist, and inventor Leonardo da Vinci (1452-1519) made notes and sketches everywhere he went. More than 7,000 pages of his sketches have survived and can be viewed in museums or in private art collections.

Ideas for Drawing

To get ideas for drawing, study everyday things and think about what makes them different, special, or interesting. Notice that most everything is **composed** (kuhm POZD) of one or more basic shapes.

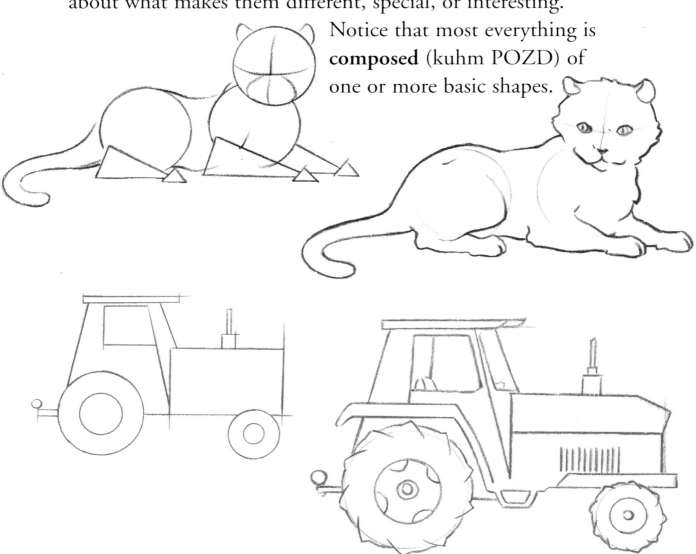

Try This

Stand far back from a house, a school, or another building and squint to see the basic shapes that make up the building. Using your finger, trace in the air the shapes that you see— squares, circles, rectangles, triangles, ovals. With a pencil, draw and connect these shapes in your sketch pad, keeping in mind that you can erase lines or parts of lines later. Pay attention to the different shapes and sizes of the windows and doors. Notice the roofline. Are there trees or bushes around the building? Once you have outlined the building using your "basic shape vision," add all the details you wish.

No Two Drawings Are the Same

There are no hard rules about drawing or creating art. Because no two people see the same thing in exactly the same way, every picture you draw is your own special, personal creation. You can see how things actually look in real life, and draw a version of it that looks real, or you may use your imagination to create something very different.

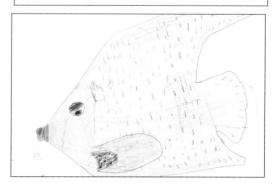

All of these drawings are of the same fish (the one at the top of the page). Each artist saw something a little bit different. This is referred to as interpretation.

Paul Cezanne (say ZAHN) (1839-1906) was a French painter who lived more than 100 years ago. Cezanne created art by his own rules. He distorted shapes and angles on purpose. Because things in Cezanne's paintings did not always look as they did in "real" life, some people thought he was a terrible artist who had never learned to draw properly. Later, people began to enjoy and understand his different vision. They began to think of him as an artistic genius and to buy his fresh, interesting paintings.

Think of a single object that interests you, say a treasure chest or a sailboat. Close your eyes and imagine it. Think about the basic shapes and lines that make up the object. Now, put your pencil near the center of your paper and begin drawing with your eyes still closed. Do not lift your pencil or open your eyes until you have finished your picture. Open your eyes and see what your "mind's eye" has created.

CHAPTER 4

Drawing People

Creating Faces

STEP 1 Start with an egg-shaped head. You may change the shape of your face by making the chin rounder or more square, but be sure not to make the top of the head flat.

Eyes are located about halfway between the top and bottom of the head. Lightly draw lines on the head to use as guides.

STEP 2 Pencil in the nose halfway between the eyes and the chin.

STEP 3 Place the ears between the eyes and the bottom of the nose. Draw the mouth, positioning the bottom lip halfway between the nose and the bottom of the chin. Add lines to indicate the neck.

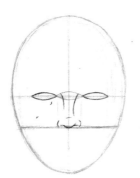

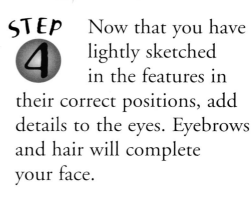

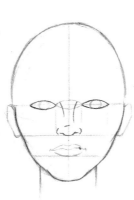

STEP 4 Now that you have lightly sketched in the features in their correct positions, add details to the eyes. Eyebrows and hair will complete your face.

13

Focus on Eyes

Drawing eyes is not hard. Draw both eyes, one after the other, in steps as explained below.

STEP 1
Draw two almond shapes, leaving a space the width of one eye between them.

STEP 2
Add lines for the irises, pupils, and the "corners" of the eyes.

STEP 3
Eyelids need to be drawn in next.

STEP 4
Add eyebrows and lashes.

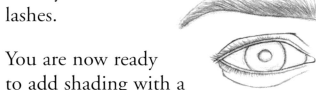

STEP 5
You are now ready to add shading with a regular pencil or colored pencil. Notice the darker areas on either side of the nose and the **highlights** (HI lits) in the eyes. You will learn about light and **shade** (SHAYD) on pages 22 and 23.

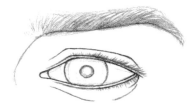

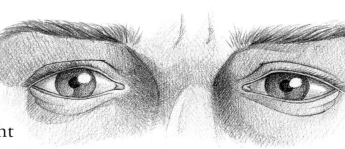

14

Noses and Mouths

By using what you have already learned about basic shapes, you shouldn't find it hard to draw the following in the steps shown.

Remember to study the text about light and shadow on pages 22 and 23.

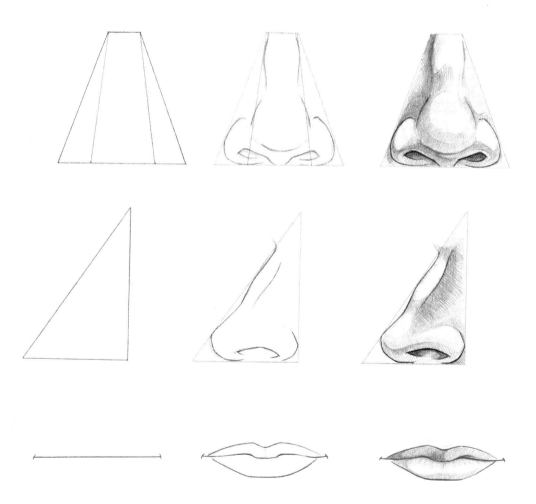

The Body

Study someone closely, using your basic shape vision and notice how the human body is made up of a series of shapes linked together at the joints. Follow these basic steps:

STEP 1 Start with a stick figure using circles to indicate where the joints would be.

STEP 2 Flesh it out with basic shapes for the arms, legs, and torso.

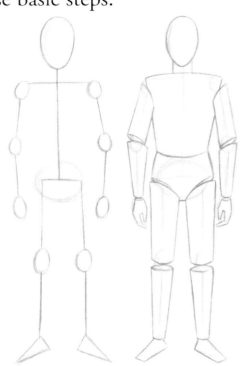

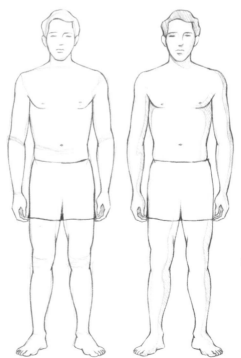

STEP 3 Now outline the body over the rectangles and circles, and put in details. Erase the lines you don't need as you go along.

STEP 4 The body can be given more **dimension** (duh MENT shun) with shading (see pages 22 and 23).

Using your basic shape vision and following the same steps discussed on page 16, you should be able to draw figures in any position—even figures in motion like this one.

Hands and Feet

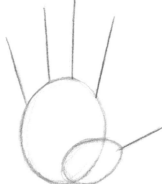

1 Start with a circle and an oval for the thumb. Draw in the five finger lines, taking note of their lengths, as shown.

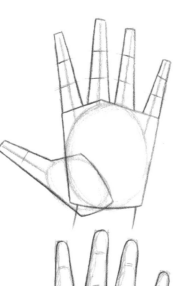
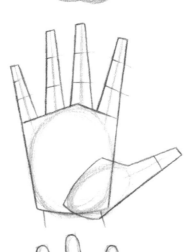

STEP

2 The fingers will look like long tubes tapered at the top. Each finger will have two joint lines and a line where it attaches to the main part of the hand. Draw in the beginnings of wrists.

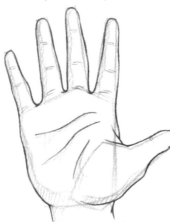

STEP

3 Round out what you've drawn so far, erasing any lines you don't need. Curve the thumb outward. Add palm lines.

 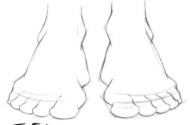 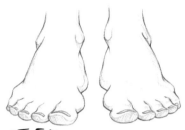

STEP 1 Human feet at this angle will be wider at the bottom. Draw in two guidelines where the toes will begin and where the joints will be.

STEP 2 Curve the toes outward. Note the relationship between the big toe joint and the inside heel.

STEP 3 Erase the joint line and add toenails. Complete your sketch with shading.

 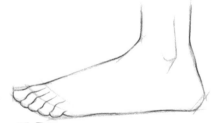 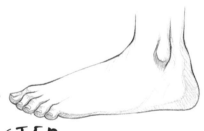

STEP 1 The foot will be about three times as long as the ankle is wide. Note how the top of the foot slopes up to join the ankle. Sketch in toe joint guidelines.

STEP 2 Add a hint of ankle bone. Sketch in the toes, sloping down at the second joint.

STEP 3 Erase guidelines. Add greater definition to the ankle bone. Round out the flesh on the toes and add toenails. To add dimension, complete your sketch with shading.

CHAPTER 5 Perspective and Viewpoint

If you view an object up close, it will appear larger than it would if you looked at it from afar. This is a rule of **perspective** (pur SPEK tiv) and it must be respected if your drawings are to have dimension.

Another rule of perspective says that the **horizon line** (huh RIE zuhn LIN), where the sky meets the land or sea, is always at your eye level, no matter where you are. If you are seated on the ground the horizon will be low. If you are perched in the top of a tree, it will be high.

Objects in your picture meant to be in the foreground should be drawn larger and in front of the horizon line; objects in the background of your picture will be smaller and closer to the horizon line.

The part of an object closest to you will appear larger. Notice how the front of the truck looks large while the back appears smaller and smaller as it gets farther away from your view.

This sketch shows a train track running through a tunnel. In real life, the tracks would be the same size and distance from one another, even though they must be drawn smaller and closer together as they go away from us. Notice that the tracks disappear altogether within the tunnel.

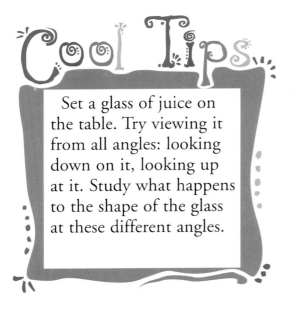

Cool Tips

Set a glass of juice on the table. Try viewing it from all angles: looking down on it, looking up at it. Study what happens to the shape of the glass at these different angles.

CHAPTER 6

Light and Shadow

As light falls on an object, a **shadow** (SHA do) is created. Where the shadow falls depends on what direction the light source—such as a lamp, the moon, the sun—comes from and how high or low it is. Look at this cube and sphere. Do you see that the lightest parts of each object are at the point where the light source first hits them? At the points farthest away from the light source notice shades (*on* the objects) and shadows (cast *by* the objects.)

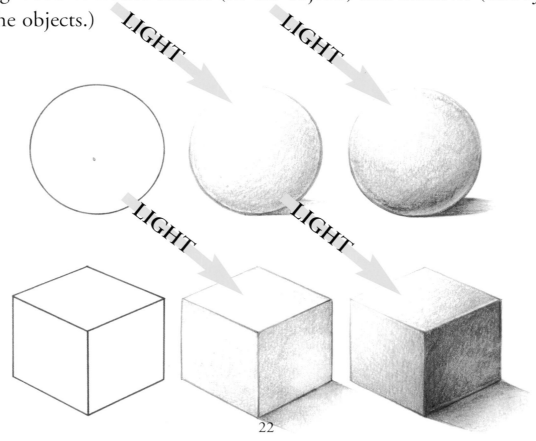

You can use the flat side of your pencil lead to create shades and shadows. The effect you will get is like the spheres and cubes on page 22. Below are more shading techniques you might like to try.

Hatching

Hatching (HACH ing) involves drawing a series of lines close together that run in the same direction. Draw more lines that are even closer together in the areas meant to be darker.

Cross-hatching

Like hatching, **cross-hatching** (KRAHS hach ing) involves drawing a series of lines running in the same direction, then crossing these with lines running in the opposite direction.

Stippling

Stippling (STIP ling) uses tiny dots or dashes drawn very close together. The closer together they are the darker the shading will appear.

Smudging

Smudging (SMUDJ ing) the lines you draw with your fingertips will fill in white areas and create a shadowy effect. It's easiest to smudge lines drawn with a soft-leaded pencil.

CHAPTER 7

Using Colored Pencils

Colored pencils come in a wide range of colors and are used in much the same way as standard pencils. The best ones have thick, soft leads that cover areas smoothly and erase well. Experimenting with colored pencils is easy and fun and they won't make a mess.

Colored pencils have sharp points, making them ideal for adding small details.

You can create some interesting color mixes with colored pencils by hatching and shading in layers. Don't forget that yellow + blue = green; yellow + red = orange, and so forth. Notice that very few things you draw are flat with only one color.

No one said pencil drawings must be soft and pale! If your colored pencil leads are soft enough, you can add deep, vivid colors to your sketches.

Water-soluble colored pencils allow you to "paint" over the colored lines that you draw. The colors spread and blend as you add water with your paintbrush.

25

Try Drawing a Plane

Using **guidelines** (GID linz) will help you effectively sketch objects at a tilt. By doing this, you can keep all angles straight and one part of your sketch lined up with another.

STEP 1 Using a straight edge, draw guidelines that form the basic slants of the plane's lines as it sits on the ground: the body, the propeller, the wing, the tail. The visible wheels will be basic circles.

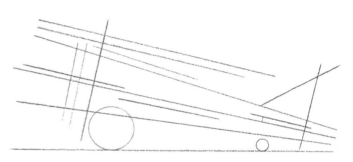

STEP 2 Use the guidelines to begin adding details to the plane. Erase parts of lines you don't need. Draw a second circle inside the larger front wheel.

STEP 3 Round out the outside lines of the plane, noting the notch for the seat. Fill in the body of the plane with color. Use shading techniques to add a metallic look to the plane's front and tail.

26

Try Drawing a Bird

STEP 1

Draw a circle for the head and an **elongated** (eh LAHN gat ed) oval for the bird's body. Draw a line down the middle of both to help you with the tilt of the bird. Sketch in a nice-sized beak, angled downward. Draw a line to indicate how the tail feathers will extend down from the body.

STEP 2

Add a series of ovals that will represent the layers of feathers and the bird's wing. Connect these ovals with another line down their middle. Connect the head and body with curved lines as shown. Add the bird's feet and square out the tail.

STEP 3

Soften all the outside lines and add detail for the feathers. Add the bird's eye. Curve the beak. Add shading with the lead of your pencil turned sideways. Erase areas you wish to highlight. Complete the bird's feet.

Try Drawing a Horse

STEP 1

Begin with a set of curved lines in the center of your paper. Make these curves into a bean shape.

Add a neck that is more narrow at the end then add a head. Draw lines in for the legs, with circles to indicate the position of the joints. Draw in the hooves.

STEP 2

Begin to flesh out the body of the horse, erasing lines you no longer need as you go along.

STEP 3

Add the mane, the tail, the eye, and the nose. Turn your pencil on its side, hold the pencil lead down with your fore-finger and shade in the horse's coat. Use your eraser to add highlights to the body, neck, and head.

28

To keep your drawings safe and **unmarred** (uhn MAHRD), you should mount them like this:

STEP 1

Choose a board that is larger than your picture with at least 2 to 3 inches all around. The board should be at least as stiff as cardboard. With a pencil draw light guidelines where you would like your paper to be mounted on the board.

STEP 2

Turn your paper face down and apply glue at each corner. Be sure to apply enough, but don't press too hard!

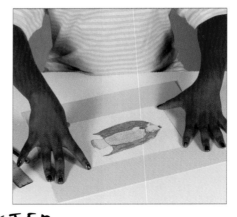

STEP 3

Use the guidelines you've drawn to position your art on the board. Press gently. Now it's ready to be stored!

Glossary

crosshatching (KRAHS hach ing) — crossing small, closely
    spaced lines over one another to create texture and tone

composed (kuhm POZD) — to form the substance of

dimension (duh MENT shun) — a lifelike or realistic quality

elongated (eh LAHN gat ed) — stretched out

guidelines (GID linz) — lines that help one when drawing
    angles or other lines that need to be straight

hatching (HACH ing) — drawing technique that uses small,
    closely spaced lines running in the same direction to create
    texture and tone

highlight (HI lit) — any of several spots in a drawing that
    receives the greatest amount of illumination; the lightest spot
    or area

horizon line (huh RIE zuhn LIN) — in a picture, the place
    where the earth meets the sky

papyrus (puh PIE ruhss) — ancient writing material made from
    soaked, pressed, and dried reeds

perspective (pur SPEK tiv) — a method of showing two or three
    dimensions on a flat surface

shade (SHAYD) — a dark value of a color; shading is on an object, as opposed to off the object like a shadow

shadow (SHA do) — dark area cast by an object when a light source shines upon it

stippling (STIP ling) —dabbing or dotting to create texture and tone

smudging (SMUDJ ing) — rubbing the marks made by a soft medium like charcoal with your finger, a tissue, or other object to create a smudging effect

textured (TEKS churd) — having visual or tactile variations; not smooth

thumbnail drawing (THUHM nayl DRAH ing) — a small-sized sketch without much detail included; a thumbnail is good for capturing an object to draw in more detail at a later time

unmarred (uhn MAHRD) — without imperfections or defects

Index

Further Reading

• Brookes, Mona, *Drawing with Children*, G. P. Putnam's Sons, 1996.
• Cummings, Pat, *Talking with Artists*, Simon & Schuster, 1992.
• Cummings, Pat, *Talking with Artists Vol. II*, Simon & Schuster, 1995.
• Kohl, Maryann, *Preschool Art*, Gryphon Press, 1994.
• Martin, Judy, editorial consultant, *Painting and Drawing*, Millbrook, 1993.
• Martin, Judy, *Sketching School*, Reader's Digest Association, 1991.
• Martin, Mary, *Start Exploring Masterpieces*, Running Press, 1991.
• Thompson, Kimberly Boehler and Loftus, Diana Standing, *Art Connections*, GoodYearBooks, 1995.
• Vaughn-Jackson, Genevieve, *Sketching and Drawing for Children*, Berkley Publishing Group, 1990.